THE MORTGAGED WIFE

THE
MORTGAGED
WIFE

Barbara Harr

THE **SWALLOW PRESS** INC.
CHICAGO

Published by

The Swallow Press Incorporated
1139 South Wabash Avenue
Chicago, Illinois 60605

LIBRARY OF CONGRESS CATALOG NO. 77-112871

Grateful acknowledgement is made to the following
magazines and publications in which many of these
poems, several in different versions, first appeared:

*Approach; Beloit Poetry Journal; Chicago Review;
Choice; Epoch; Gallery Series/two; Harper's; Jeopardy;
Literary Review; Michigan Quarterly Review; Minne-
sota Review; Northwest Review; Poetry Northwest;
Poetry Review; Prairie Schooner; Sage; Saturday Re-
view; Shenandoah; Aphra; Tri-Quarterly; New Poetry
Anthology I* (Swallow).

My thanks also to the Poetry Society of America for the
Alice Fay di Castagnola award (1965) which eased my
way. And my thanks to Yaddo for the summer of 1967.

And kneel and say an Ave there for me

                          And learn to bear
the burden of the tenderness
that is hid in us

As though, in tempests, peace were found!

CONTENTS

IV. VARIATIONS

I

FLAGSTONES

The Mortgaged Wife

Here in the Hopper Highlands
the houses wave with flagstones
and whirlybird-sprinkled lawns

as the whistle from the platform
sings the seven-o-seven
straight to the Loop the loop

where he signs his name, his endorsement
of this check in check out
receivable weekly.

Ostensibly for the League of Women Voters
or Marching for Dimes
I hit the streets.

My book is full of Green Stamps
stuck with hope and spit
redeemable for premiums some day.

Next To The Godly

In the pink place
next door to the laundromat
where the coffee is thick and hot

we met once more and drank
to the tenderness and ironies
of the pure in heart.

You said, stay a while,
our work will wait.
But I got up to go,

paid the exorbitant check,
and said that my clothes were clean by now,
my dimes' worth done.

my shirts and diapers dried
of sweat and remnants,
the ginger touch on the back of the neck.

I left, and felt
the chlorine taste of detergent on my tongue
and bleach in my bones.

The Raccoons

Every night of the honeymoon
they came to the cabin window,
their thin black fingers
begging for bread and meat.

He laughed at them, that first night,
and tossed them crusts of bread
found in the back of the ice box,
blue, crumbled hard.

He tossed them a crust or two
then let the window fall
barely missing her fingers
on the window sill.

Prohibitions

I.

When Grandpa, like Luther, nailed the rap
On the indulgent cops of Kansas City,
Damned demon rum and published from the pulpit
Names of the brothers of the paying order,
The bootleggers, the officers, the mayor,

Struggle and love he knew, but never pity
For self or syndicate. He told his story
With documented gospel-facts; ignored
Martyr-omens pinned upon his door,
Bulls *ex cathedra,* promising in stages
Concrete cassocks, one-way pilgrimages.

Bible in mind, he braved the bootleg mob;
Faced sawed-off muzzles, barrelled through the bluff
Of men whose loaded customers and dice
Made speaking not so easy; broke down doors
With G-men at his heels; collected bones
And bottled relics, bits of evidence.

The hoodlums came—came one, came ninety-five.
By faith alone my grandpa stayed alive.
Let other saints fight Roman, demon, dragon;
He put the city on the water wagon.
And till they shrined him under Kansas sod
His only thesis was the word of God.

II.

Meanwhile his not-quite-cloistered oldest daughter
Could pitch a curve in hardball, ride a mustang,
Make speeches, love and cocoa-fudge; could pull
Jerusalem through a holy slide trombone
Until old ladies wept in prayer-meeting.

Depression summers, she worked the national parks.
Loaded for bear, she hit the peaks; inveigled
Trout from the lake and silver from the tables.
Played for the dudes, and danced a bit, and smoked,
And bluffed a drunken fisherman to love her—
Purely, of course—also the boys at church camp.

Tipping the purse just right, she broke her way
By streetcar through the local Quaker college.
Majored in math, too broke to study music.
Quick but untriggered, she tried her rifle mind
At small-pond frogs, but never found a target
Worth telescopic sights. She ricocheted,
Chipping a bit the walls of old cathedrals,
Back on herself in a quarry of uncut thoughts.

At graduation, staring the depression
In its lean lip, she married a good man.
After five years he bought her a piano
And after ten, a car. Deliveries
Came from the Jewel Food Store every week,
The obstetrician every year or two.
She gave her children Testaments to read,
Alice in Wonderland, Beginning German,
And Richard Wright with the dirty words inked out.

III.

At forty-eight she modified her vows:
Went on a diet, practiced typing faster,
Bought a Picasso print, a book of Bartok,
And hung a new can opener on the wall
For her good man. She worked her married daughter
Quietly through a Radcliffe Ph.D.

And sent her second son, a shiftless sort,
Around the cutting world by cattle boat,
Oxcart, Berlitz, and bluff. Paid his way

7

Through years of pounding paper pads and pavements,
Concrete images, telescoped horizons,
And printed no's from third-rate magazines.
Through two divorces and a year in jail;
Through faith and works. Until his book came out:
The family pride, in ninety thousand words
Nailed on the broad door of the universe.

Because She Is Leaving

Because she is leaving
she will cook a breakfast
grand as his mother used to make.

Burned with five years' words,
the two of them will try today
the taste of ordinary things:

syrup too sweet, too slick,
stab of trees in a dark wood,

jelly of strawberries
almost ripened, almost to seed,

butter, fat of the land
that disappears in a yellow streak

and the spitting guts
stuffed with the butcher's leavings,
shrinking on the fire.

When the food is done
she will wash the dishes—
store the ones he will not use,

and leave, for days, in the dry house,
the smoke of too-hot skillets,
of cakes too fliply turned.

To My Children In Darkness

I had my chance at you
but banished you with numbered days
and married folks' devices.

Now, as I quit this house,
I see you down the years:
black-haired children, lovely as his sister,
or classic-plain as me,
stubborn as little mules, or lost
in dream worlds of your own,
scribbling love notes, fighting after school,
howling in church.

And standing behind you, colder,
knowing all my mind,
the little bastards of my dreams
begotten soft upon me
by men of words and music.

When I am ready to marry,
no one perhaps will need
the paper-fingered crone
of twenty-nine years.

New Year's Inventory

I have no lover
but eight pet cats

and one mad friend

and one who thinks (ha ho)
I am his wife

Drum Song: For A Leave-Taking

Feather-head waters, love,
split on these rocks
and flay our hide canoes
to matchwork.

In the dog days
the buttered hills
beyond our deep ravines
drop nourishment as water.

White-water torrents say
far off where berries rise
and apples walk on water,
the sky is falling.

Silver Gate

I.

The bull moose looks
with his glass eye
down from the wall above the hotel bar
upon the rows of bottles
and lady-statuettes.

This moose with weathered horns
fought in a rising stand of flesh
for a cow, or the first rights of the herd,
and won, perhaps, or lost.

He is scarred by horn or cutting hoof,
shot, pellet, the vermin of these walls,
and watches with a twist of heavy lip

as the Pack Rats and Gearjammers
sitting around the bar
ogle the waitress, wriggling by
in tight pants and pony tail,
her white felt Stetson, leather belt
and tray of steins.

A bearskin, silver-tipped,
covers half the other wall,
shifting shades in a flicker
of brown and gold from the firelight.
Her skin is lined with dugs
turned these years to leather.
She was shot through the head and skillfully patched.

II.

Jo, the waitress, dressed
in deerskin and a cotton shirt,

is off work now. She leans back,
her hair blending in bearskin.

On the ranch she broke the ice
from the kitchen water bucket
for her good man, at twenty-three below.
In summer, swept the dust of tumbleweeds
blown through the cracks of her house
out through the door.
And when her man brought home the deer,
she cleaned it, cut it up
and smoked it on a spit
basted with sweetness.
She caught, cleaned, gutted
the pink-rose trout
that flicked her rod in the stream.
She learned to swing a rope, helped tie
the calves in branding time,
wrestled a bull-calf to the ground
and held him there hurt
while an iron fired the leather alive
with the brand of ownership.

She is twenty now,
does not believe in divorce,
but sits here on the lap
of Dago John.
His hand moves on her breast.
He is singing a sad song
and feeding her Chianti.
The accordionist comes over,
smiles, follows the tune.

She feels the box of music
squeeze and expand.
Ice in a bucket is cracked apart;
rose wine guts her heart;
and sap in the burning logs
spits sweetness.

III.

Mornings, across the lobby,
she works behind the counters.
Dressed as a cross-breed Indian girl,
she lets her dark hair hang.
She is slim in a squaw dress
trimmed with silver rick-rack.

Her goods are souvenirs.
Here in a case lies silver
cut and wrought to filigree:
loops for a wrist or ankle,
a bauble for a pulpy ear,
a drop-weight on a chain.

Blankets she has, woven soft
from warp to tapestry,
warmth to cover a brave's bed
or wrap in wilderness colors
his woman's waist.

The dudes come off the highway.
A woman mauls the baubles,
holds up a turquoise
to her doughy chest. Her friend decides
this blanket will not do for Sally Ann
who drapes across her sofa
too damn much junk already.

Antlers hang on the walls,
skins, a fish or two,
a scalp in braids, another hacked off short.
A child touches one,
asks his father,
was this a man or woman?
"Don't touch that thing," the mother says.

Jo brushes by. A college boy,
shifting a hip and shoulder,
pins her against the wall.
He stretches one hard hand
under her dress. She pulls away,
walks behind the counter
through the door marked "Ladies."
She tries to hold the door shut.
It will not stay.

She is tired. She would like to walk
into the hills and not come back.
She has heard the wild things
crying for the moon,
and in those hills, among the grasses rising,
pigweed, indigo, bugseed, love-lies-bleeding,
she remembers a flower that cannot be touched . . . .

The customers are gone.
She runs her fingers through
the silver of the till:
dimes, a few dollars.

Deathwatch

All night in underworlds
we talked, and banished
old judgments, errors
and halfway-images.

In Gothic vaults
from bar to floating bar
came Aphrodite rising among foam
schooners of glass and gold.

Until we spoke
of the last register
where names are written down
and all men lie.

There in the panic woods
the ancient gods are blown away
and hailstones fall about
Our Lady of Regrets.

stroking the same cat
our hands touched, like folded
wool, or silken under-
things from the dryer

once, a child, I scuffed
across the threadbare rugs of
an old house, on a dry day,
deliberate, in anticipation

but the cat slept,
soft, white and gelded,
running out of lives

Saint Patrick's Eve

Sandra, lady, mother, wife of sorrows,
I remember your green jumper
the first day of school.
You made a mess of the finger paints.
I didn't tell. We were friends.
Later that year, our teacher
explained Saint Patrick's Day.
The day of the Irish: not a day
for gifts or resolutions,
but a day for a sort of frolic,
just before spring, before green things sprout
and sweetness rises in the trees.

At eight or nine years old, Sandy,
we dug in my daddy's garden,
got our hands dirty, and loved
the warm touch of the earth.
We tried my mother's recipe
for crumb cake with sweet topping,
but used, in error, the rancid lard,
and could not eat our cake.
A few years later, we stuffed
our undershirts with socks,
trying for cleavage;
we tottered in borrowed heels
and envied girls with shapes.
Older, we double-dated.
You fixed me up once
with a wrestling team from Iowa.
The evening was a fiasco.

All the while, we sang:
first Whispering Hope in the junior choir,
gospel choruses, ladies' barbershop,
Mother's Day music for the Garden Club,
Holy Week cantatas.

In high school we came to the harp of Tralee
where Irish eyes were smiling,
and slightly with a wicked eye
we flirted through the garden where
the praties grow.

Until with older judgment
we loathed the professional Irish
stereotypes. We even tired
of the lusty drinking and wenching songs
of Makem and the Clancys.
Irish potatoes were tasteless;
whiskey made us ill.

I have come back to this cold town:
my marriage like a rack of knives,
yours on the brink.
Here in your kitchen, your children asleep,
your husband on the road,
we sit and drink.
You get a telephone call
from your almost-lover, and stare
at peelings in the rubble of the sink.
After a while you cry
and pour martini mix
in a big schooner.

We talk of this suburban town:
white, anglo-saxon, Protestant,
moral and middle-class;
and the city of our paychecks
where Keane and Daley run the machine.
Paddy says, in the 43rd ward,
Chicago ain't yet ready for no reform.
This morning, at the commuter train,
you passed the ad for the Holy Name.
On coffee break this morning
I browsed with laughter through a rack
of insult greetings, little bright cards

printed on orange paper:
"Happy Saint Patrick's Day, you Irish bastard";
and in the corner, in small print,
the label, "made in England."
We turn to ribald tales of priests and nuns,
to men confessing adultery
and easily absolved.
Or you cross a baboon with an Irishman,
and what do you get? (a stupid baboon)
You tell me of the Notre Dame men in your office
who always win at the football pool
and sleep with the stenographers
as well as the lady heads of Personnel.

You pour another drink, and one for me,
and tell me of your office friend,
the Irish salesman with the blarney tongue
who tells you that he loves you.
You are afraid to sleep with him.
He took you the other night
just as far as the bar
on the first floor of the hotel;
and he told you today over cocktails,
this abstinence is killing him.

I listen. Your words strike me with a clang
of recognition. Alarum. Dublin's burning.
In terror for myself and mine
I will not speak of things like this.
My tongue is like potatoes
but I think that you see through me.
I drink, and cry with you, and look
into my own martini.

You tell me how your dad,
honest dealer in dry goods
and other stable wares,
worried for your young honor
until you were safely married.
I think of mine, the minister,

most nervous at my wedding.
We are drunker now,
and both of us think but do not speak
of all the married Irishmen
who may before the end of Lent
confess us through the slats.
What will they have to do, do you think,
to wipe us from their souls?
A word, a flick of beads?

The silence screams in Gaelic.
We go to the piano.
I pick an Irish folk tune, and you laugh.
We search your pile of music
for something we can sing with comfort,
something we know by heart.
We rummage in the sheets
of notes that weave about the lines
and find the classic Franz
that we both know, die grossen Schmerzen,
machen die kleinen Lieder.

You fumble at the keys.
We sing in German; I explain,
happy with my knowledge,
that the man who wrote these words—
poet, Jew, Protestant fake—
was more unhappy than we, but at least
not Catholic, though he married one
and led her a hell of a life.
We sing, but are off pitch
from alcohol or tension.
Your fingers miss the keys.
We give it up as a lost cause,
but still the room is music.

The cuckoo on the green wall strikes—
midnight, and we are pumpkins
before the ball.

It is Saint Patrick's Day, a day
for celebration.
Our glasses gone, or empty,
we raise our union cards
bright with love and insult.
Happy Saint Patrick's Day, you Irish bastard!
In famine and rebellion
we sing the harps and shamrocks of a faith
that tries to hold a marriage
leafless, unstrung,
untuned and out of luck.
Our swollen roots are dug,
uprooted, out of starch.
A thousand pikes are marching
at the rising of the moon
and we are lost in the foggy dew . . . .

The room turns quiet. Good old Pat,
who drove the snakes from Ireland!
We find them here on the walls
and trace them with our fingertips, unblinking.

(also for J. J. McM.)

I curled at your feet, that night;
we talked of loss and marriages,
the words of humankind
that came to us too late

when we were grown, were trained
to tricks in hoops and cages.
My pet, we choose the whips
of our own three-ring minds;
we beg the world for its canned bones,
its broken spines to catch our throats.
Love, we belong
not to the keepers of our tents
but to the claws that mock us.

You prowled out alone, then,
into the reeling city,
town of calliopes and clowns
and bareback girls.
I cried, that a sleeker beast
with harder jungles in her limbs
might feed you her red meat and bones,
strike you off to sparks
and love you half as well . . . .

I went away on my soft feet
and found in a vacant lot
the steel machines of people.
I drove a long road slow with fog
home, to be petted and fed
and gently put to sleep
with gas, or the shot of a needle.

Wounded Euridice

(Corot)

I.

Her hair is brown in a classic coif
bound with a cord or tie of red

The lights on her falling robe
and from her shoulder
slide down her slender arm
to the point of her wounded foot

A speck of light settles on her bare knee
carelessly out of the drapery

Something red lies by her on the rock
and an indecisive white flower or two
sprout by the rock where her dress slips down,
the dubious rock or log.

II.

Girl, don't just sit there
looking at your hurt foot!
Have you the tools or guts or wit
to suck or slash,
cut yourself clean,
take to your mouth the curse of snakes
by your own action?

Orpheus won you, as he must
win all men with his art.
But Hymen's torch, at your marriage feast,
smoked, and brought tears to your eyes.
The priests and processions are gone now,
your bridesmaids too are gone,
and neither your husband's name nor strength of art
could forestall this bite, or heal it.

Your poison and your need
are in your own blood.

Girl, will you never learn
to walk your own way from death
without limping or leaning?

III.

When he comes
to darkness for her sake

(Is it not enough
to be so loved?)

will she not choose to follow,
or dare to stay,

but simply take his hand again
and limp half way to light

while he, knowing well
her ways, her mind,
turns back in doubt?

IV.

Who gives a prick for the bitten?
In praise of Orpheus,
In sorrow for his loss,
Men's poems all are written.

V.

About that bite, Euridice—
it caught you running away
from the man whose hives of bees were later to spring
alive, by the help of the gods,
honey from carrion, for his forgiveness.

II
RIBBONS

The Seafarer

*(Man should be just within the bounds of his social order, but
when he ventures out on the high seas of human relationships,
he is sure to be shipwrecked, and then all he can do is to save
himself by clinging to love.*

—Martin Buber, *Tales of the Hasidim: Later Masters*)

When I was a child
learning to walk,
I rode across the sea:
my mother was seasick all the trip
and my father soon exhausted
following me on sea-legs
exploring up and down.
He pulled me back from the rail
and put me on a leash:
he got the whole idea
from another passenger, first-class,
who kept a pet monkey.

I had no choice of sailing.

Now I am told, as children
are told by old seafarers,
it is the sea that rises
with life-bearers to the moon.
But the sea is full of muscled sharks
quickly drawn to the wounded.
And shipwrecks happen all the time:
even the best-inspected
threshers of government,
with regimented crew,
burn in the deep.
Many brave souls are rocked
sunken hull to hull
in a Sargasso of love.

And is it true, my sweet,
that lust and love are one?
Saint Paul would not say so.
Paul was shipwrecked too.
He was saved, and God knows why,
for his words of good advice
(be subject to the authorities;
you shall not fulfill the lusts of the flesh;
it is better to marry than burn)
have caused us so much trouble—

Scuttle, my love, the broken ship,
the worm-eaten, rusted,
battered, barnacled hull.
Break out the lifeboats, jackets,
and cling to a spar.
Abraded by the saving raft or spar,
we may wind up
torn in a muscled maw
or else our bones made coral
in a sea-change.

Is it so bad, after all,
to be a part of the sea
(pearls that were his eyes)?
For sirens long have sung
their magic songs.

And it was Peter, not Paul,
who walked on the water—
Peter, the impulsive, quick-denying
and first-affirming—

Sailor, save yourself—

In love, I dream
of walking on the water
or sinking in a cry of grasses moving—
no longer alone.

Fragments After Sappho

through white screens
the light of birds
woke me

when love jostled me on the sidewalk
he had a field jacket on

I have bought flowered sheets
in case you should come again

writing letters
is a losing game

("Poetry should be oratory or song . . .
    the colloquial is nothing . . . "
                    —E., comment on a poem)

i.

I would be poetry to you,
but will not bobble pebbles
over a sea, a mob of men
swaying in each opinion's tide.

I will not stump the grass roots,
print my face on billboards
or enter into great debates
with makeup and hot lights.

ii.

Perhaps I am closer to song,
but barely have the backing
for a break, a riff of instruments
improvised by ear.

For I have little wind or brass,
and sound percussive only
in the snares and kettles of my heart,
the strung drums of my skin.

I could sing a plainsong
out of a lost tradition,
and aria off the top of my head,
dry recitative

scarcely audible

iii.

I would be poetry to you,

but would rather be a woman
with smudgy hands and crinkly hair
and the plain speech of my feelings.

I would persuade with common words,
with the lines of my rough tongue

echo small words in your head.

Conversational Fragment, With Afterthoughts

I. Fragment

The two of them walked on the ice,
skidded and spattered by taxicabs.
"Are you insured?" she laughed.
"I'm worth more dead than alive," he smiled.
"Not me," she said, "but I told them
to give me to the medical school,
a slap in the teeth at death—"

II. His Mind

I think of joints and structures,
beveled planes of form and bone,
the replicas, the fiddles
and gongs of her young body
curled on a couch, or moving
in one man's bed—

My wife, my child, my mistress,
keep you forever—
let no checkered angels
take you on slipping streets,
let no antiseptics
of hospitals or schools
fall upon the ringlets
and drums of your pale body
under the knives
of the laughing boys.

III. Her Mind

I cannot claim or insure
your time or your feelings
but gamble my life in interest
in this indemnity

and play with words, with policies
written on shredded paper
to cancel out the terror
of worth.

On this black ice, I hold your cuff
and know the premium of loss,
of silver slipped away,
as I grow old.

Rapid Transit

A mile away, the subways rise
into the light, and move among
the leaning stairs of tenements:
close to a quarrel in a house,
children at supper, worn-out loves
asleep behind a broken shade.

I called to you, one evening,
across a subway station.
You could not hear, and shrugged aside
my last words of the night.

Sweet, we were born to eat, to sleep,
perhaps to dream a while,

to ride where blind men tap
their tin cups down the aisles
with songs of love and death,

to run, packed into crowds
where loonies touch our thighs
or doors close on our fingers,

to punch a transfer home
up the stairs of signboards
unpatrolled, alone.

Returning Late Past The Subway Shops

I ride the vaulted tunnels home,
having left the man
whose word can leave my tongue
a petal torn of lies.

The florist's stall is closed.
A dim light warns the few
who would be thieves of flowers.
Cornflowers, here, for the poor,
roses for the solvent,
and all degrees of blossoming
(I have loved gardenias
just for their brownward turning
about the fingertips)—
orchids, purple at the throat,
padded wet in cotton.

Blocks from home, I count the stems
kept till another trading day
when young men may be richer
or honest girls may buy their own.

Locked, in the night, these flowers
are each man's own to take.
And they are mine to count:
my ice-box full of roses.

Walkup

I climbed the stairs to your room
with no good reason in my head.
They were plastering the walls,
painting the railings drunkards hold
or children take in a flying leap
to land in a heap below.

I have clung to rails that splintered in my palm
and moved up other stairs, defaced
with swear words in three languages;
passed the crossed-off scores of games
and how-to-do-it diagrams
of love and the act of love.

I brushed your walls, in passing,
and did not note till later
the blue and white on my brown coat:
an old coat, but it kept me warm,
pockets and lining shredded out,
its maker's label lost.

This dust will not brush off.
I wear you on my sleeve
and on the hard part of my hand.
(I might have been more cautious
and climbed a cleaner stair.)
My coat is marked. I do not care.

Armistice

Early December. You told me to go:
you did not want to bring
trouble to my life.

The sweet words of diplomacy
had not hid scraps of cutting iron.
I had those hours to kill.

I walked along the piers,
watched the soldiers load
machinery for defense;

found a friend, and told him
a few old strategies of yours;
dropped asleep a while.

On waking, I recalled
through a blue haze of gunfire
you, and Pearl Harbor Day.

Love At The Political Crisis

Here on the summit of the night
our talk is done
and panic buttons pop.

I am disarmed: reserves are gone.
Old blockades are broken.
All holds are open.

As men dig in
their daily bread and water
the world's flesh burns.

We with a touch forget
our homes, the friends we love,
and all the schools that taught us,

then watch the small rains fall
on green fantastic growing things
in cities without song.

Letter From A Cribless Field

Since you left with the snow
I walked through these long acres
where dry ears grow.

Blackbirds crackled
to the empty stalks
at the fence's end.

A silk wind blew
leaves in my skin
and all my hair was tassels.

Almost alone, a lady may
forget the touch of snow
only a blade away.

Envoi

In that café
it was my hand of fire
that closed about a globe of candlelight
and shone, my flesh transparent,
thin on the twigwork of my bones.

Rose of light, of blood
that nourishes my marrow,
move at a thought's touch
to him who spins upon the world,
rootless in Eden.

Tell him what we a moment knew:
though candles light our hands
on burning seas,
and others glimmer east and west,
flicker, go out,

These broken globes may be the ones
that light us to the deep
in a far land which neither of us owns:
floating lamps and loves
light through our bones.

The Catholic Cemetery, Next Door

Once more inside my childhood house,
I can look out through gravelled gates
upon that ground where Catholics
carry a last approval seal
to Peter of the keys.

When I was little, I would watch
the great stone landscaped Christ
at cemetery's center.
The squirrels ran among his evergreens.
I cleared the dust from crumbling stones
of oldest graves in foreign tongues:
Im Friede, Ruhe.
Noted the graves of children
(a little boy in my class
caught lockjaw from a rusty nail,
died, and was buried there).
Explored the grotto's winding stairs
of porous rock
and once, caught in a summer rain,
curled half-dry in a niche
beneath a virgin's arms.

With friends, I ran and hid
among the brush
of the downward slope beyond the graves
and pulled the crimson sumac leaves
that turned each fall.

When I was a child, I prowled the heap
beyond the hill, beyond the Christ,
and picked the ribbons of the dead
from wilted wreaths,
made little dolls, and houses,
and trimmed my hair.
My hair, in ribbons, blew
to crow-song in the piney wind.

Older by years, I walked or ran
where tracks of black or brighter cars
with all their headlights on
ran yet to darkness on a gravelled road,
where niches slipped and rain blew in;
lightning fell in sheets;
weathered virgins stood with broken hands.
My tongue was trimmed and split
like crows' feet in my head,
rattled like crazybones in sleep,
and every stone was carved
in a strange tongue.

These winter months have brought me far
with your indulgences.
Your words were grace, your touch
translated peace,
pried loose the jaws of silence,
unwound my path and held me on the slope.
Breaking the tapes and wires of years,
your hands ran in
like ribbons in my hair
and black birds, white birds, flew.

This morning, in the sun,
snow gives up the ghost
in dark patches, under the trees.

Bless me, love,
through green and rocky days,
through touch and resurrection.

III

SARGASSO

III

SARGASSO

Upon A Name

In Nigeria,
in the dark of the rainy season I was born
with no anesthetics, and my mother said
"A woman's a fool to go through this more than once."
The chief came to my father and said
(paraphrased from the Hausa)
"A girl? Too bad, old chap."

And I cried.
They called me Barbara, the stranger
(but the chief called me Mazakha for his mother).
They shot me full of quinine for the fever
and took me on to Liverpool
as befitted a missionary's daughter.

Barbara, foreigner,
what world is this?

Clean Sweep

My great-aunt, small and wiry,
clean to her Methodist bones,
would come to stay with us.
She wielded stick and broom and rags,
her recipe for godliness.

She took my bed, swept my dresser bare
then rearranged it, spread it
with her unearthly goods.
There were the pills for her flashes,
the long rat for her hair,
her Bible, stamps, marking pen,
a horn box for her combings.

She swept through my young mother's house,
ransacked our deepest closets, burned
our toys and souvenirs,
ordered and straightened out
my mother's sweet wild kitchen shelves,
pinpointed all the fruits turned sour,
the rose-gold pungent peaches
subtle with molds of green and gray
in their clear jars.

She made me help her. She and I
scrubbed down the house.
My mother—who had read to me
of the tongues of men and of angels,
of godmothers, and love—
drifted, her furious dust
shattered and bright in the sunlight.

Tonight in the dust of a rented room
I try the tongues of angels
but hear the cymbals clang

in the sounding brass of dustpans
I will not touch.

Mother, cinder girl—
clear out this dust, these rags
oily with age, these firetraps.

The Member Of The Locker Room

My father coached the team.
The year they won the trophy,
I was twelve. At every game
I kept the score in chalk:
my father's win or loss, my own
handwriting on the wall.

Sometimes I played, at practice,
and the boys laughed.
I learned the tricks: the lay-up,
jump, shuffle and rebound,
to pick up a pass, take tip-offs,
heed the man with the whistle.

Then I went on alone
to a hard-bench locker room
where I soaked my toes in chemicals
against pernicious growths
and scrubbed my hair, my knobby head
in the spigot-spray.

But I was not yet dressed
when the room turned full of swimming girls
in petal-ruffled suits.
And I, a bare child, thin in my bones,
turned awkward from their laughter,
their flesh, their talk of lovers.

Fall Talk

Gym-shoe summers, we played at warriors
Or bandits in the woods. We played and fought
With pigtail-pulling little boys, evaded
Indians, Al Capone and Chinese spies
And mothers wielding combs and home-made soap
When pine-pitch snarled our hair.
                                    We fed raccoons
In moonlight, brought the baby porcupine
Home in a thick wool jacket that prickled for weeks.
When the wind was loose, we heard the timber wolves
Trailing a crippled deer at the edge of the swamp.
And the bulldozer plowed out a bear, raking, rearing
Black before the machine. Not far away
Was hidden island where Dillinger hid out
From the F.B.I., for years, in luxury.
And the grown-ups said, if there was another war,
Here was their hideaway. A man could live
Fishing or berrying. And even death
Moved in warm flesh, crying, unmechanized.

Summers have passed. The cabin is painted white.
Poachers leave, in the tall grass on the point,
Empty shells of cartridges and a world.
With spray net in my hair, I in Chicago
Eat chop suey next door to the Biograph
Where Dillinger was shot.

Breakaway

Father, your roots and solid ground
saddle, hobble, clip us.

Held by the bit and blindered,
I worked your field your way,
then in the furrow scratched the sides of earth
with gravel in my nails and in my knees
and dust of fertilizer in my mouth,
all out of step, and tangled in
your harrowing discs.

Father, your loving fences stun
but do not stop
my kine, bull-headed.

My white birds will not beat
their feathers on the henhouse wall
but keep their heads

and when the fox is free
in dust and wheels
will take their chances running on the road.

Advice From The Ward

Watch out, kid,
for those who cherish you,

who glue your mind in shining tiles,
hide from your hands all cutting things,
bind your thoughts in gauze,

who love too well
your small brain scrubbed and glazed.

At The Zoo

The snow-leopard cub
bounces
three-fourths air

and children
note with delight
his little tummy muscles
are pudding, fluff or angel-cake—
a cotton-wad body,
whipped cream with smudges,
the milkweed tuft,
a snowball rolling mushrooms

as the old one
rasps the red flower of beef, then
blood pounding to her teeth
stalks the merry gapers.

A Weight Of Parables

My father's house has mansions
but also barn doors shut
on skittering fillies set to run away—

dead-water ponds, and greenish fields
where kindly shepherds watch the one
who goes astray.

Father, I leave. I have laid up
my treasures in the valley of the shadow
where moths break chrysalis.

I will know the weasel,
the eagle in a shock of cloud,
the white surprise of fox.

I fear the wolves will walk
among the straw and feathers of your barns
a day before we die.

Power

The pale girls break
like watermelons
on the front of your face.

Watch the pink flesh crumble,
seed lie spit on the ground,
green shells crack.

The American Children

Dead men, in Manila Bay,
rose to the city's nets.
Photographs were posted:
family or friends could claim
flesh for a grave and candles.

The children of diplomacy
passed on their way to school,
scribbled on the pictures
and thought of pigs or Grandma

and later, much later,
asleep on a swollen ceiling
or in a fat manhattan
saw their own wet flower-faces
drown.

Clark Street

A crooked block from home, the gay boys go
past derelict buildings waiting for the wrecker

where the poignance of improvement blows about
like litter in March wind. The city's money
ends aberration, sets up family housing.

Under these steps no children play. The doors,
lockless, boarded blind eyes, stare. Stiff shades
chatter like cold teeth in broken windows.
Chalk-scrawled walls, between obscenities,
hold shredded faces of unelected men.

Before the fall, I should like to have gone inside
the flats and passageways where men have lived,
seen the turnings of their ways, and gained
the unexpected knowledge of the dead

before the swinging ball, from chain, from crane,
in its diminishing orbit, brings the end.

The Vulture Tree

(Lincoln Park Zoo, Chicago)

i.

Food, a perch, a drain,
concrete only dimly stained
with marks of meat or blood.

Turning, the birds nuzzle
stubble-feathers of their wings,
one's eyes flat pursuing.

Once in the wild, this bird
would kill the hawks, the hustlers
who paced him for his food.

Here every day, at sunset,
he lifts his wings, heaves, jerks,
hits the wire, and settles
back for another day.

Aimed by a famine in the brain,
he shoots
at the pale flank of the sky
and misses.

ii.

Great bird, wild bird,
I think of you in Big Sur
or on a Western plain
over the hulks of buffalo
swelling black, the white man's waste,
over a cow, her unborn calf
still quick inside, and kicking,
your bone beak dipping

over the helpless dead,
your beak dipping tenderness
in the soft parts of the dead.

iii.

Old bird, this morning
before the dew dried, and the sun
lit the tall buildings over Lake Shore Drive,
I quicked my breath and caught
at a moving thing
creeping among my feathers.

It clicks now, is caught,
the itching thought,
blood-sucker in this vein
of my pumped heart
ticking away the cold blue water
trying to be blood.

Bird, your white eye
grips in a dream of egg shells.
Your bone beak clenches
the shells of parakeets
chattering cold blue nonsense
in the sweet tongues of people.

Dear bird, this bareness
cries in my mind
like a barked bough, like driftwood
scoured, without leaves.

I am watching you,
brother-bird, watching me:

prey for a thought, a broken shell,
or a bit of flight by violence
beneath my wings.

The Search

I will not take your way
after the white mole truth
whose eyes are blind.

I think his fur is cold;
his scent is musk.
He has strong teeth,
leaves mocking droppings in his path,
and white fragile bones
of all small animals.

I will not think, you say.
I think you will not see
the worlds of earth about.

You work your wires of thought
and lethal gas of logic.
Your terms shift earth
and halves of living things
cut by your spade
lie damp and white.

I fear your cry
far underground
where small bones line
the China-plunge to error.

Sargasso

Weary again with reading,
I think of eyes:

I see the black, hardened eyes
or some great hungering bird
that dives, eyes open, after solid prey

of those of a flounder
lacking much bulk of body

seeing just one side
of these wet weeds of thought.

Port of Call
(to G., on the stories of his travels)

I dream I walk
your ordered, torn,
razored foreign quarters.

I may be mocked,
short-changed, shanghaied
by ragged toughs who know their game.

A red dust soils these streets
where priests in yellow robes
hold empty bowls.

As hands move, under cloaks,
the touching of the bone reveals
beggars and others, poor in love.

You hold a child in your arms:
I try to shape, through my own eyes,
her image into truth

and through the temple ruins
pick out the painted shapes of men,
the uncut forms of women.

Poetics
(for Philip Beaurline)

The tales I told at fifty cents an hour
To pop-eyed children six or eight years old
Upheaved the total baby-sitting trade
And crushed the competition. The bedtime epics
Accompanied by pablum and the bottle
Were masterworks, immune from Aristotle.

Pity, purgation, plot—such spectacle!
There was Quicksilver Pete, and Angus the kind Apache;
The moose who married a cherry tree and raised
A family of hatracks; the centipede with corns;
And Stephen Hero, who saved his little sister
From a gigantic blob that rolled like a spoonful of jello
Eating bad children. He saved her, swept her away
On the back of a flying horse called Pegasus
To Axel's Castle, where they lived happily
Except for Lord Weary who snored too loud in the tower.

Sometimes, in a pinch, a dialectic effort:
"What do you think happened next?" "It ate him!" "That's right!"
And on till the time the gopher burrowed a hole
Under the covers, like so, lights out, good night!
Leaving them flabbergasted but in bed.

I answered an occasional mystified query
From frantic parents, confused by a phrase or a jingle
The children had chanted ritelike all week long.

These were the triumphs: weekly re-engagements
With Attic chants as I walked in the door—
"Tell us a story!"
                              But one distrustful child,
Inscrutable mind behind small leopard-freckles,
Refused. "No, don't tell me that.

I want a *real* story, something from a real book.
Something printed, with pictures, on real white paper."

Fiercer than teachers, child, more coolly decisive
Than editor-critics—you have torn up my poetics,
Scoffed at mimesis, verisimilitude,
Energy rhythms, suspensions of disbelief.

Your paper standard of values will last, perhaps,
Until you have learned to smoke. About then you may find
That ink runs thinner than truth, and thinner even
Than hot air distilled from ink.
                                    But now, for the moment,
As you sit happily holding your real live book,
My formula fails: my tongue and my pen are water.

When I was in the tavern
(just to be there when he was there)
I laughed, to catch his eye.
He gave a toast to the ladies
but none at all to me.

He never called till the end.
Why did he stoop to dramatics?
One word could have made me trust him.
Who knows what might have happened
through these ten thousand dawns?

What was it that he died of?
Why did he make me a dying joke?

Juana: *Guitarist*

I was those fingertips
    turning harmonies
by a river   two days before war

a woman, a guitar
(river is chilly, muddy, cold,
walk that lonesome valley)

blonde-topped wood
inlaid trim   geometries
measured silver frets

gut and silver steel
stretched to tension in the pegs
action barely touching

what hills what hills are those, my love?
mine eyes have seen   frosty morning
coral of the Solomons

if there was not war on the radio
there was death all around us:
wars in our fingertips

tenting tonight   the small rains down
cruel war is raging   may I
go with you   no

I am gentle sounds beside water
away you rolling river
bound away   before war

she died of the fever   her ghost wheels
alive alive   o   cruel death
give these things back   the dancing bones

these chord-changes

The Lute Girl's Song

("My disciples, why do none of you study
the *Songs?*" Analects XVII.ix.)

My mother, long a widow,
won from the emperor
a chastity gate, inscribed
to her honor. Before she died
she left me her lute, long silent,
and the books of my father.

All night in the western room
I read the writings of K'ung.
But my lute made a twang
and shivered the blinds.
I lost my place in the book.
How shall I sing, I wondered,
and follow the teachings of K'ung?

That summer I played my lute
in the emperor's court
and golden lions rose
at the touch of my song.
Afterwards, in the shadows,
I asked the scholars
for answers.

One only blinked.
"Seek first of all," he told me,
"the teachings of K'ung,
and your songs will heal the heart."
Another was silent a while.
Then, "I have taught my daughters
all that I thought was right.
But my fingers are stiff now,
my lute is out of tune,
and music has left my head."

In the far province of Ch'in
where the houses rise like mountains
I sought a wise man.
He sat on his mat and listened
a while to my song.
"How shall I play," I asked him,
"and follow the teachings of K'ung?"

He placed me on his mat
and kissed my mouth.

("The people of Ch'i sent to Lu a present of female musicians,
which Chi Hwan received, and for three days no court was
held. Confucius took his departure."   Analects XVIII.iv.)

The Dresses

(for Kathleen Fraser)

Those gifts in place of preacher's pay:
potatoes ours for the digging;
chickens we had to pluck and gut,
pinfeathers sticking our fingers;

and the styles of ancient women
altered to our young bodies.

Kathleen, we are permitted to keep
any mystery or brightness
that lasted through the blueing.
Those dresses have surprising tensile strength,
more threads than you think, to the inch.
We can steam-iron over wrinkles
or crush them harder and tie the knots
for our own coloring
in op or pop as we please.

Or knot them into firemen's ropes
swung out of open windows
when parsonages burn.
Swinging to our own kingdoms,
a blister or two on our hands, no more;
then freedom, our feet on the ground.
Free to dance, to sing those songs
we couldn't sing before.

We know by now
that air- and water-walkers use
illusion or technology.
Our highest flying
may be our swinging from those rags
knotted into ropes

and strung from stained-glass windows.
Swinging like Tarzan (no, we Jane)
from vine to thorny vine
far away from home
with jungle leaves in our hair.

Folk Lament

From my feather bed and ring for every finger,
I had heard of English bells,
of cherry blooms and stories without end,
moonshine hills and huckleberry wine,
High Germany

sad bells,
what will you give me?

I am tired of dreaming
of foolish things.

In a cellar bar with candles and guitars
we sat and sang at closing time
and the tables danced like Hasidim
for a red-headed Czech and a missionary's daughter.

At the Small World, at three o'clock today
the drinkers did not know you

I sat on the steps
and walked the street, uneasy
(say the sad bells of Swansea)
and waved, mistaken, at a passing stranger.

Songs, be forgotten
in the dregs of closing time,
for the cabin boy has had her child and drowned,
and cherry trees do not bow down
for Christ or virgins,
bum again.

In weariness of dreams
and ignorance of motives

my head
was seventeen come Sunday.

Juana: *The Burnt Foot*

cooking   inattentive
spaghetti-water for supper
steady   without a sieve

blazing soft   wrinkles
shooting rods through the body
oily   tight

hold   crush the ankle
leg between the burnt spots
ice bucket when brave enough
out   rested   back in

pink rose bumpy flesh
skin wrinkled   draperies
thin white dead   graceful curves
pulled   fallen together
dark rose patch pulled tight about
high hard blister   deep water
skin purse full of gold
slides under surfaces
a hand can move it about
arches   gristle
thin ankles rising
axle rods   camshafts
spine sprouting out of them
roots to the ground   balance

pressure or it's lost
cut the shoe   it falls off
stays   caught in gratings
knocked behind a news stand
down a subway stairs

how will she travel   how will she walk
or float on spikes through Gotham
in slippers   boots   open skins
hand-fed animals

beautiful upon mountains
anyone's feet

The Court Girl's Tale

i.

I said to the emperor's son:

I will bring you a scepter,
a signet ring of gold,
a bowl of blackening mead

and the brown hills beyond
the rivers of grief,
a folded leaf

and in the dark chamber
beyond your walls
grow grey along with you.

ii.

The emperor sent to me
sandals tied of hemp
and a walking-stick of jade.

He wrote, "I have considered
the land where you should live.
There is no place like the city of Wei.

"In Wei, the couriers say,
the pear-tree blooms are whiter,
lopped by the pruner's shears."

iii.

I stitched for the emperor's son
a quilted coat to keep him warm,
its pockets lined with double silk,
its sleeves with padded paper.

iv.

The emperor charged the Lord of Ch'in:

Go to the mountain country,
with my black horses matched and trained,
my name on your chariots, my sign
on all your banners.

Go to the mountain country:
make blazing the towns and castles
that my lands may be at rest.

v.

Here in the mountain country,
in the city of Wei,

in the city of Wei—

Final Week

(Spring, 1967)

My people, I leave to you
this deck with the aces missing.
This butterfly gone from the hands,
four bullet holes in Charlie.
The shoe recovered from Mother and pain,
a sweet French violet tintype,
a mug with seven faces
growing out of clay bark.
Comic-strip balloons to blow your minds
and one pack of invisible
morning-glory seeds.

I leave you steering upstream
on the back of a stuffed red herring
with only a fin for an oar.
Remember, the world is a tree growing upside down,
rooted only in sky.
You will have to fight through mistletoe and orchids
and other parasites
clogging the way of your hands.
You must loop-the-loop
through narrow streets in Helena
(is it the streets or the buildings that slant?
flip a coin, and we'll see).
Or beat Aztec gold into feathers,
recalling always the thinginess of things
and proving a gain in the ample size of the sample.

I leave you the TV commercial with love
lasting all 24 hours.

IV

VARIATIONS

The Victory Statue

(variations on a theme of Zbigniew Herbert's)

I. Nike

Forces roll before her.
Most of the men who cry to her
are beyond her help:
the weights already cast, the scales falling.

Those who will be victors
simply assume she is present.
(If she were gone, they might sense that
something was vaguely missing.)

II. Nike Who Hesitates

She notices a solitary man,
that one beyond the others.

Knowing his battle record
she counts him above the generals.

He seems a man of two faces:
one very young, one aging gray,
shadowed by branches in ruins.

A chance word, a gesture
cuts through stone.

     ❀   ❀   ❀

She sees him move on the track of words
into unholy clashes.

Crossing country mud
supply lines are broken.

In this new world
his maps are incomplete.

He must jolt his lines
into foreign cogs and cartwheels.
He works with tin and baling wire;
his chariot pitches him on.
Nike aches with him at each bounce of the road.

✿ ✿ ✿

Nike would terribly like
to go up
and kiss him on the forehead

However
he might, as she knows, then choose to live,
betraying those who claim him, who trust him to die;

or else
he might not recognize her—what would he think—
this crazy lady blundering into trenches
bothering men when they're busy
fixing an axle or loading a gun in haste

✿ ✿ ✿

Had she touched him, he might have been gentle
(more likely, only puzzled)

It is safer to stay in character
as people and gods have taught her
("You are marble: do not move")

✿ ✿ ✿

It is hard to be
a woman of wings, but of stone—
the weight and flight pull hard against each other.

There is little for her to do.
Today's wars leave no winners.

She feels so heavy, in marble.

III. Nike of the Earth

She loses gravity.
Somewhere a gray cell says: Release.

Her shoulders somehow soften.
A frazzled feather falls to ground.

Veins in marble begin to run blood,
seeping out at the chisel marks.

Wings go limp, disintegrate,
flake off like the old skin from a blister.

Clusters of wrinkles, at finger joints,
shift to fit the bending.

Her feet are stronger than she knew.
She can run on this bare earth.

The raised veins run blue blood, some pink.
She can feel it move and shift and bump
in rhythm with her heart.

Her tongue undone from stone can speak, can sing
no longer patriotic hymns
but the revolutionary songs of earth,
of love and bread and flowers.

A man in the front line calls to her:
not a prayer, not a command.
He speaks to her, mortal to mortal.

She has some strength on this earth.
She puts her shoulder to a cart.
The people in the wagon track

break a crust with her, curse her for slipping,
take her for one of themselves.

Death may come, or it may not.
She does not worry now
but touches wood, drinks sour cheap wine.

Ideas of gods have killed so many people.
We have no more to spare.

She will find food; the people somehow do.

❀   ❀   ❀

Un Bel Di

in memoriam: Marilynn Mitchell Olsen

i.

In my walkup room on east Ninth Street
at zero point   between First and A

my mother telephones

she tells of the cord in your closet

Home from the hospital
in that suburb of Milwaukee
with your parents   not with your husband.
You leave two little children.

She knows no more to tell me

ii.

We were eighteen together.
On the Mission to Youth
we traveled, saving souls.

In that Protestant school, we settled down to college.
Your black-browed singing teacher, furious
when you hummed in for a lesson,
your short curls tipped with ice
from the swim and the run uphill.
"What is this cold, this wet?
You should keep yourself in a hothouse!
You will major in music, of course?"
                       No.
We sat in the sewing lab and talked.
Food for the hungry nations

was the dream of your young years—
you with the voice that stunned us.

iii.

We were Midwestern
good girls of the fifties.
No pot, no pills, no protests—and where has it got us?
A quirk of your face made you seem to be always smiling.
Some people misunderstood:
saw you only as the track-meet queen
loved by handsome athletes.
You sang the standard freshman arias
of Mimi and Cio-Cio-San.
In that time-punched dormitory room
we cried for the young evangelists we loved.
You sang of the dim and the dark cloths
that those boys trod upon.

Then, realistic, we married men who loved us:
you wed the handsomest athlete;
the brightest theologian married me.

You sang at my wedding: through shadowed vale
my heart will fear no ill.

You left school, left us all. From that time on,
if you sang, I never heard you.

Should we have gone to Thailand
with garden seeds in our packs,
sewing-machines and culverts in our ship-holds?

Was it our dreams that were wrong?

iv.

Un bel di. That workhorse. I tucked it away.
Even on records, no one sang it like you.
Until, years later, Vishnevskaya
at Philadelphia Hall.

Her scheduled program closed
with Moussorgsky's Songs and Dances of Death
(very few women can make them work;
they need a basso's power).
Her husband, the famous cellist,
accompanied her by heart,
almost conducting, leading her with love
on an instrument not his own.

After the applause,
with armloads of roses lifting over the footlights,
and the man I then loved best
shouting Russian bravos in the aisle
(he is married now, to a beautiful black girl),
me with a cough, hoarse and getting hoarser
as my voice followed noiselessly along,
past the program's end,
floating up through golden rings of people,
the thread of smoke rising,
her unexpected encore, high note sudden
opening   un bel di

v.

In this far city, my red pills
calm me for work or sleep.

I play again the tapes
(your music was the best thing at my wedding):
the Lord's my shepherd, I'll not want;
entreat me not to leave thee

and the disc, our college choir.
You come in, shy, on the solo soprano part,
Laudate Dominum.
We all come in on the chorus, and I cry, No—
the glory was not in the father, son,
the glory was in the young woman
who sneaked one breath before that long last cadence.

You hold beyond us all.
The Amen is yours alone.

vi.

I think, *Marilynn, Marilynn,*
we would all have taken care of you.
No, we could not.

If I still had our rags of heaven
I would spread them under your feet.
You walk over all of us now.

Was it the traps of all our promises
to God and men
that sprang on you too soon?

Girl, the click of your throat.

vii. (*Ballade of Dead Ladies*)

McCullers. O'Connor. Hansberry.
Jayne of the bosom, car-crash dead.
Kilgallen cracking the Kennedy case.
Lurleen, little sick governor.
Anne Frank. Viola Liuzzo.
Addie Mae Collins. Piaf.
Francesca Cabrini on mule-back.
Sylvia's oven and her bees.
Marilyn Norma Jean.
Ferrier, Song of the Earth.
Lady Day of the blues.

Mary of sorrows. . . .

viii.

Marilynn, *un bel di—*

84

We have seen him on the Pacific
coming for us, his white sails high—
God, or a young evangelist—
I no longer know who he is—

the proper Victorian lady by his side
offering our children a life of sorts
but little for our own souls

our swords the only custom and ceremony

I will not go down to meet him
You could at least have let him climb the hill

(Precious Lord, take my hand, we sang)

Blessed your tender broken chords
Blessed your frozen curls
Blessed the breath you caught

Ghost of Marilynn, sail past the blade,
the crossroads, the rope sprung tight

Be to us white sails
in the hours of our life

Let us keep the music of our pulse-beats

*   *   *